Basil Brush™
BOOM★BOOM

Ho Play

Basil

Bingo

Mortimer

Based on the original Basil Brush animations
Illustrated by Bill Ledger
Story adapted by Clare Robertson

Basil and Mortimer wanted to play.
"What can we do?" asked Basil.

"We can have a race," said Mortimer.
"We can have a horse race."

"A horse race will be fun," said Basil.
"Is there a race track?"

"Yes," said Mortimer. "We can
have a race there."

"Hello," said Bingo. "Can I race too?"
"We can all race," said Mortimer, "but
I will win. Bang! Bang!"

They went to the race track and got on their horses. It was time to race!

"On your marks, get set ...
GO!" said Mortimer.

"Hey!" said Basil. "You went too soon."
"Oh well," said Mortimer.
Mortimer was winning.

Bingo had a plan to make his horse run faster.

He took out a carrot and put it on a string. Bingo's horse was hungry so it ran very fast!

Soon Bingo was winning.
Basil was at the back.

"This is not good," said Basil.
But he had a plan ...

... a rocket!

"Look at me go!" said Basil.

"I am the winner!" said Basil.
"Boom! Boom!"